Walking the Bridge of Your Nose

Selected by
MICHAEL ROSEN

Illustrated by CHLOË CHEESE

Kingfisher

NEW YORK

KINGFISHER
Larousse Kingfisher Chambers Inc.
95 Madison Avenue
New York, New York 10016

First American edition 1995
4 6 8 10 9 7 5 3

LIBRARY OF CONGRESS CATALOGING IN PUBLICATION DATA
Rosen, Michael
Walking the bridge of your nose / Michael Rosen;
(illustrated by Chloë Cheese,) — 1st American ed.
p.   cm.
Includes index.
Summary: A collection of limericks and other humerous poems,
arranged in such categories as "Mouth Manglers," "Silly Patter," and
"Tombstone Tomfoolery."
1. Children's poetry, English.   2. Nonsense verses, English.
3. Humorous poetry, English.   [1. Nonsense verses,   2. Humorous
poetry, 3. English poetry.]   I. Cheese, Chloë, ill,   II. Title.
PR6068, 068W35   1995
821',914 — dc20   95-3007 CIP AC

ISBN 1-85697-596-7

Edited by Caroline Walsh
Designed by Chris Fraser
Printed in Spain

CONTENTS

Acknowledgments

The publisher would like to thank the copyright holders for permission to reproduce the following copyright material:

R.O. Brierley: R.O. Brierley for "Oodnadatta" by R.O. Brierley from *Stuff and Nonsense* (William Collins Pty. Ltd., Australia 1974). Copyright © R.O. Brierley. **Dave Calder**: Dave Calder for "Where?" by Dave Calder. Copyright © Dave Calder 1992. **William Cole**: Curtis Brown Ltd. for "Foolish Questions," an American Folk Rhyme adapted by William Cole from *Oh, Such Foolishness!* selected by William Cole (J.B. Lippincott). Copyright © William Cole 1978. **Gina Douthwaite**: Random House U.K. Ltd for "Nuts" from *Picture a Poem* by Gina Douthwaite (Hutchinson 1994). Copyright © Gina Douthwaite 1994. **Willard R. Espy**: Harold Ober Associates Inc. for "Private? No!" from *Another Almanac of Words at Play* by Willard R. Espy (Andre Deutsch 1981), copyright © Willard R. Espy 1980, and for "Reverse Verse No. 7" from *The Game of Words* by Willard R. Espy (Bramhall House), copyright © Willard R. Espy 1971, 1972. **David Harmer**: David Harmer for "Riddle Me Wrong" by David Harmer. Copyright © David Harmer 1993. **John Kitching**: John Kitching for "My First is in . . ." by John Kitching from *My First Has Gone Bonkers*, edited by Brian Moses (Blackie 1993). Copyright © John Kitching 1993. **J.A. Lindon**: The Estate of J.A. Lindon for "Sink Song" by J.A. Lindon from *Yet More Comic and Curious Verse* (Penguin Books Ltd.). Copyright © J.A. Lindon. **Eve Merriam**: Marian Reiner for "Misnomer" from *Chortles* by Eve Merriam (A Morrow Jr. book). Copyright © Eve Merriam 1962, 1964, 1973, 1989. **Ogden Nash**: Curtis Brown Ltd. for "The Jellyfish" by Ogden Nash from *Verses From 1929 On* (Little, Brown & Co. 1959). Copyright © Ogden Nash 1942, renewed. **Louis Phillips**: Louis Phillips for "The Long Sought After Proof." Copyright © Louis Phillips. **Jack Prelutsky**: Greenwillow Books, a division of William Morrow & Co. Inc. for "The Cow" from *Zoo Doings* by Jack Prelutsky (Greenwillow Books). Copyright © Jack Prelutsky 1983.

Every effort has been made to obtain permission to reproduce copyright material but there may be cases where we have been unable to trace a copyright holder. The publisher will be happy to correct any omissions in future printings.

Introduction

Ever since there has been language, people have played with it. Archaeologists have found funny rhymes scratched on the walls from ancient Roman times, and all over the world people have made up tongue twisters, riddles, puns, and all sorts of wordplay. In this collection I've tried to bring together different kinds of games that English-speaking people have played with words. Sometimes we know who did the playing, like Ogden Nash, Eve Merriam, or Jack Prelutsky, but often we don't know, and a funny rhyme or a riddle has just grown up among a group of people, and somebody, luckily, came along and wrote it down. So when you read this book, be prepared to be baffled, bamfoozled, bewitched, and bedazzled. Either your tongue or your mind may be twisted up and whirled around in circles. Just hang on to your seats and wait for a giggle.

MICHAEL ROSEN

Esau Wood sawed wood.
Esau Wood would
saw wood.
Oh, the wood that
Wood would saw!
One day Esau Wood
saw a saw saw wood
as no other woodsaw
Wood ever saw
would saw wood.
Of all the woodsaws
Wood ever saw saw
wood, Wood never
saw a woodsaw that
would saw wood
like the woodsaw
Wood saw would
saw wood. Now
Esau Wood saws with
that saw he saw saw wood.

10

THE COW

The cow mainly moos as she chooses to moo
and she chooses to moo as she chooses.

She furthermore chews as she chooses to chew
and she chooses to chew as she muses.

If she chooses to moo she may moo to amuse
or may moo just to moo as she chooses.

If she chooses to chew she may moo as she chews
or may chew just to chew as she muses.

JACK PRELUTSKY

Once upon a barren moor
There dwelt a bear, also a boar;
The bear could not bear the boar;
The boar thought the bear a bore.
At last the boar could bear no more
The bear that bored him on the moor;
And so one morn the bear he bored —
The bear will bore the boar no more.

You've no need to light a night light
On a light night like tonight,
For a night light's light's a slight light,
And tonight's a night that's light.
When a night's light, like tonight's light,
It's really not quite right
To light night lights with their slight lights,
On a light night like tonight.

"Night, night, Knight," said one Knight
to the other Knight the other night.
"Night, night, Knight."

Sheila Shorter sought a suitor;
Sheila sought a suitor short.
Sheila's suitor's sure to suit her;
Short's the suitor Sheila sought!

Down the slippery slide they slid
Sitting slightly sideways;
Slipping swiftly see them skid
On holidays and Fridays.

SILLY PATTER

OODNADATTA

Oodnadatta
Parramatta
Names to make your tonsils chatter —
Tonsils chatter,
Silly patter
Oodnadatta
Parramatta.

RONALD OLIVER BRIERLEY

Did he say I said you said she said that?
He said you said I said she said that!
Well, I didn't!

There were two skunks —
Out and In.
When In was out,
Out was in.
One day Out was in and In was out.
Their mother,
who was in with Out,
wanted In in.
"Bring In in,"
she said to Out.
So Out went out
and brought In in.
"How did you find him
so fast?" she asked.
"Instinct," he said.

SINK SONG

Scouring out the porridge pot
Round and round and round!

Out with all the scraith and scoopery,
Lift the eely ooly droopery,
Chase the glubbery slubbery gloopery
Round and round and round!

Out with all the doleful dithery,
Ladle out the slimy slithery,
Hunt and catch the hithery slithery,
Round and round and round!

Out with all the obbly gubbly,
On the stove it burns so bubbly,
Use the spoon and use it doubly,
Round and round and round!

J.A. LINDON

Our Joe wants to know
if your Joe will lend our Joe your Joe's banjo.
If your Joe won't lend our Joe
your Joe's banjo,
our Joe won't lend your Joe
our Joe's banjo
when our Joe has a banjo!

A fly and a flea flew up in a flue.
Said the fly to the flea, "What shall we do?"
"Let's fly," said the flea.
"Let's flee," said the fly.
So they fluttered and flew up a flaw in the flue.

NURSERY CRIMES

Hickory, dickory, dock
Two mice ran up the clock;
The clock struck one —
But the other one got away.

Mary had a little lamb,

A lobster   and some prunes,

A glass of milk,   a piece of pie,

And then some macaroons.

It made the busy waiters grin

To see her order so,

And when they carried Mary out,

Her face was white as snow.

Old Mother Hubbard
Went to the cupboard
To get her poor dog a bone.
When she got there,
The cupboard was bare,
And she said: O I C U R M T!

Liddle Mees Muffitt
Saa Tonner Tufford
Eaton Herr Corzon Waye
Winn Alongo Kammer Spyra
Unda Sathe Down Beese Eidher
Ann Frydmann Mies Muffitt Taw Way.
(Compiled from the Toronto Telephone Directory)

Humpty Dumpty sat on a wall,
Humpty Dumpty had a great fall.
All the king's horses and all the king's men
Had scrambled eggs for dinner again.

MONTEZUMA

Montezuma
Met a puma
Coming through the rye;
Montezuma
Made the puma
Into apple-pie.

Invitation
to the nation
Everyone to come.
Montezuma
And the puma
Give a kettle-drum.

Acceptation
Of the nation,
One and all invited.
Montezuma
And the puma
Equally delighted.

Preparation,
Ostentation,
Dresses rich prepared:
Feathers — jewels —
Work in crewels —
No expense is spared.

Congregation
Of the nation
Round the palace wall.
Awful rumor
That the puma
Won't be served at all.

Deputation
From the nation,
Audience they gain.
"What's this rumor?
Montezuma,
If you please, explain."

Montezuma
(Playful humor
Very well sustained)
Answers "Pie-dish,
And it's my dish,
Is for me retained."

Exclamation!
Indignation!
Feeling running high.
Montezuma
Joins the puma
In the apple-pie.

D.F. ALDERSON

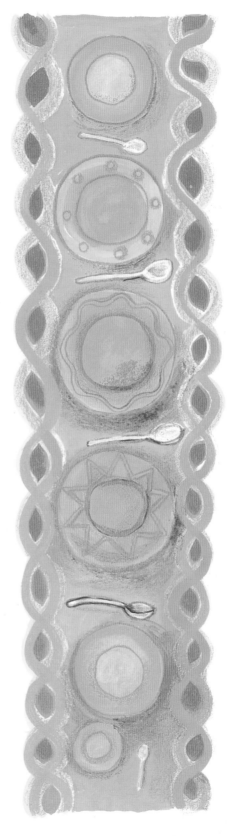

SOUND BITES

All I want is a proper cup of coffee
Made in a proper copper coffee pot.
You can believe it or not,
But I just want a cup of coffee
In a proper coffee pot.
Tin coffee pots
Or iron coffee pots
Are no use to me.
If I can't have
A proper cup of coffee
In a proper copper coffee pot,
I'll have a cup of tea!

We eat
what we can,
and what we can't,
we can.

THE JELLYFISH
Who wants my jellyfish?
I'm not sellyfish!

22

You can have —
Fried fresh fish,
Fish fried fresh
Fresh fried fish,
Fresh fish fried,
Or fish fresh fried.

Two legs sat upon three legs
With one leg in his lap;
In comes four legs
And runs away with one leg;
Up jumps two legs,
Catches up three legs,
Throws it after four legs,
And makes him bring back one leg.

I was round and small like a pearl,

Then long and slender and brave as an earl,

Since, like a hermit, I lived in a cell,

And now, like a rogue, in the wide world I dwell.

I went to the wood and got it;
I sat me down and looked at it;
The more I looked at it the less I liked it;
And I brought it home because I couldn't help it.

TOMBSTONE TOMFOOLERY

ON MRS. NOTT
NOTT BORN.
NOTT DEAD.
NOTT CHRISTENED.
NOTT BEGOT.
LO HERE SHE LIES
WHO WAS AND
WHO WAS NOTT.

HERE LIES
THE BODY OF
ANN MANN,
WHO LIVED AN
OLD WOMAN
AND DIED AN
OLD MANN.

HERE LIE
JOHN ROSE
AND FAMILY
THIS GRAVE'S
A BED OF ROSES.

HERE LIES POOR WOOD
ENCLOSED IN WOOD.
ONE WOOD
WITHIN ANOTHER,
ONE OF THESE WOODS
IS VERY GOOD;
WE CANNOT
PRAISE THE OTHER.

THIS GOLFER HERE
WOULD SWING
HIS CLUBS,
TILL TIME
AT LAST TOOK TOLL.
NOW IN THIS GRAVE
BELOW THIS STONE,
HE'S REACHED
HIS FINAL HOLE.

26

HERE LIES
WHAT'S LEFT OF
LESLIE MORE.
NO LES.
NO MORE.

JOHN BROWN,
DENTIST
STRANGER, APPROACH
THIS SPOT WITH GRAVITY,
JOHN BROWN IS FILLING
HIS LAST CAVITY.

ON EMMA AND
MARIA LITTLEBOY
TWO LITTLEBOYS
LIE HERE,
YET STRANGE TO SAY
THE LITTLEBOYS
ARE GIRLS.

STEPHEN CROTCHET,
MUSICIAN
STEPHEN AND TIME
ARE NOW BOTH EVEN:
STEPHEN BEAT TIME
NOW TIME'S BEAT STEPHEN.

OWEN MOORE
GONE AWAY
OWING MORE
THAN HE
COULD PAY.

NONSTOP NONSENSE NONSTO

A doggie stole a sausage
When he was underfed.
The butcher saw him take it
And now poor doggie's dead.

And all the little doggies
They gathered there that night
They built a little tombstone
And on it they did write . . .

A doggie stole a sausage
When he was underfed.
The butcher saw him take it
And now poor doggie's dead.

And all the little
     doggies . . . .

Why is the Fourth of July?
Because
J is the first of July and
U is the second of July and
L is the third of July and
Y is the fourth of July.
Because
J is the first of July . . . .

JULY

You remind me of a man
What man?
A man of power
What power?
The power of hoodoo
Who do?
You do
Do what?
You remind me of a man
What man?
a man of . . . .

There are three ways to get peanut butter off the roof of your mouth:
one way is to shake your head back and forth.

If that doesn't work, you could kind of whistle.

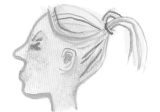

If that doesn't work, you could scrape it off with your first finger.

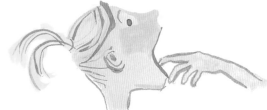

There are three ways to get peanut butter off your finger.
One way is to shake it off.   Another way is to blow it off.

If that doesn't work, you can scrape it off with your two front teeth.

There are three ways to get peanut butter off the roof of your mouth . . . .

This is the key of the kingdom:
In that kingdom there is a city.
In that city there is a town.
In that town there is a street.
In that street there is a lane.
In that lane there is a yard.
In that yard there is a house.
In that house there is a room.
In that room there is a bed.
On that bed there is a basket.
In that basket there are some flowers.
Flowers in a basket.
Basket on the bed.
Bed in the room.
Room in the house.
House in the yard.
Yard in the lane.
Lane in the street.
Street in the town.
Town in the city.
City in the kingdom.
Of the kingdom this is the key.

Anna Maria she sat on the fire;
The fire was too hot, she sat on the pot;

The pot was too round, she sat on the ground;

The ground was too flat,
she sat on the cat;

The cat ran away

with Maria on her back.

I went down to the river
And I couldn't get across,
So I jumped on a mule —
I thought he was a horse.
The mule wouldn't pull,
So I traded him for a bull.
The bull wouldn't holler,
So I sold him for a dollar.
The dollar wouldn't pass,
So I threw it in the grass.
The grass wouldn't grow,
So I traded it for a hoe.
The hoe wouldn't dig,
So I traded it for a pig.
The pig wouldn't squeal,
So I traded it for a wheel.
The wheel wouldn't run,
So I traded it for a gun.
The gun wouldn't shoot,
So I traded it for a boot.
The boot wouldn't fit,
So I threw it in a pit,
And you fell in on it.

ENGLISH CLASS

FOOLISH QUESTIONS

Where can a man buy a cap for his knee?
Or a key for the lock of his hair?
And can his eyes be called a school?
I would think — there are pupils there!
What jewels are found in the crown of his head,
And who walks on the bridge of his nose?
Can he use, in building the roof of his mouth,
The nails on the ends of his toes?
Can the crook of his elbow be sent to jail —
If it can, well, then, what did it do?
And how does he sharpen his shoulder blades?
I'll be hanged if I know — do you?
Can he sit in the shade of the palm of his hand,
And beat time with the drum in his ear?
Can the calf of his leg eat the corn on his toe? —
There's somethin' pretty strange around here!

American folk rhyme adapted by WILLIAM COLE

HINTS ON PRONUNCIATION

I take it you already know
Of tough and bough and cough and dough?
Others may stumble but not you,
On hiccough, thorough, lough*, and through?
Well done! And now you wish, perhaps,
To learn of less familiar traps?

Beware of heard, a dreadful word
That looks like beard and sounds like bird,
And dead: it's said like bed, not bead —
For goodness sake don't call it "deed"!
Watch out for meat and great and threat
(They rhyme with suite and straight and debt.)

A moth is not a moth in mother
Nor both in bother, broth in brother,
And here is not a match for there
Nor dear and fear for bear and pear,
And then there's dose and rose and lose —
Just look them up — and goose and choose,
And cork and work and card and ward,
And font and front and word and sword,
And do and go and thwart and cart —
Come, come, I've hardly made a start!
A dreadful language? Man alive!
I'd mastered it when I was five!

T.S.W.

*pronounced *lok*

36

An old couple living in Gloucester
Had a beautiful girl but they loucester!
She fell from a yacht
And never the spacht
Could be found where the cold waves had toucester

37

Write, we know, if written right,
Should not be written wright or right,
Nor should it be written rite, but write,
For only then is it written right.

GHEAUGHTEIGHPTOUGH spells POTATO.
How?
GH is P, as in hiccough;
EAU is O, as in beau;
GHT is T, as in naught;
EIGH is A, as in neigh;
PT is T, as in pterodactyl;
OUGH is O, as in though.

*Add the commas
in the right places
and this rhyme will make perfect sense.*

I saw a fishpond all on fire
I saw a house bow to a squire
I saw a parson twelve feet high
I saw a cottage near the sky
I saw a balloon made of lead
I saw a coffin drop down dead
I saw a sparrow run a race
I saw two horses making lace
I saw a girl just like a cat
I saw a kitten wear a hat
I saw a man who saw these too,
And says, though strange, they all are true.

39

Punctuation can make all the difference to meaning:

The butler stood by the door and called the guests' names.
The butler stood by the door and called the guests names.

Private — no swimming allowed!
Private? No. Swimming allowed.

A clever dog knows its master.
A clever dog knows it's master

Go slow, children.
Go slow — children.
Go, slow children.

A Consistency of Plurals

The plural of tooth is teeth;

Is the plural of booth then beeth?
The plural of mouse is mice;

Is the plural of spouse then spice?

The plural of that is those;
Is the plural of hat then hose,

And the plural of rat then rose?
Who knows?

Flim·Flam·BALONEY·&·BUNKUM~

Ladles and Jellyspoons
I come before you
To stand behind you
And tell you something
I know nothing about.
Next Thursday
Which is Good Friday
There'll be a Mothers' Meeting
For Fathers only.
Wear your best clothes if you haven't any
And if you can come
Please stay at home.
Admission free
Pay at the door
Take a seat
And sit on the floor.
It makes no difference where you sit
The man in the gallery is sure to spit.

The train pulled in the station
  The bell was ringing wet.
The track ran by the depot,
  And I think it's running yet.

I jumped into the river
  Just because it had a bed.
I took a sheet of water
  For to cover up my head.

One bright September morning in the middle of July,
The sun lay thick upon the ground, the snow shone in the sky.
The flowers were singing gaily, the birds were full of bloom;
I went upstairs to the cellar to clean a downstairs room.
I saw ten thousand miles away a house just out of sight,
It stood alone between two more and it was black-washed white.

MISNOMER

If you've ever been one you know that you don't sit the baby,

you bouncer   stander   holder   halter

puller   patter   rocker   feeder

burper   changer   kisser   bedder

EVE MERRIAM

Once an ant
Met a bat.
Said the bat
To the cat,
"Why the dog
Don't the elephant
Get the fish out of here?"

Preposterous Puns

Mississippi said to Missouri,
"If I put on my New Jersey
What will Delaware?"
Virginia said, "Alaska."

Do you carrot all for me?
My heart beets for you,
With your turnip nose
And your radish face.
You are a peach.
If we cantaloupe,
Lettuce marry;
Weed make a swell pear.

NUTS

*O*live *Fig*'s a *gooseberry*,
she's *cherry melon*choly,
her *date* has *bean* and let her down —
he ran off with a *cauli*.

Flowers could not ap*pea*se her
No, *Olive* took the *pip*,
"Such *chicory*! I am *appled*
that he should not *turnip*."

Her *passion* it waned *parsley*
when some*yam* else did *sprout*,
"You're looking *radish*ing tonight.
Floret him. Let's go out."

She's heard upon the *grape-lime*
this *mango*'s wild for her . . .
if *currant orange*ments bear *fruit*
these two won't stay a *pear*.

GINA DOUTHWAITE

A famous painter
Met his death
Because he couldn't
Draw his breath.

Doctor Bell fell down the well
And broke his collarbone;
Doctors should attend the sick
And leave the well alone.

A rabbit raced a turtle
You know the turtle won;
And Mr. Bunny came in late
A little hot cross bun!

I was going to buy my sister
a box of chocolates,
but she's on a diet.
It's a seafood diet.
If she sees food, she eats it.

Q. There's a man in a room,
without doors or windows.
The only furniture is a wooden table.
How does the man get out?

A. First of all he bangs his head against the wall until it's sore.

He takes the saw and cuts the table in half.

He puts the two halves together to make a whole.

He gets through the hole,
and then he shouts and shouts until he's hoarse.

He gets on the horse and rides away.

THE LONG-SOUGHT-AFTER PROOF that MONEY GROWS ON TREES

1. Money is what people get when they sell.
2. Sell sounds the same as cell.
3. A cell is a tiny room.
4. One kind of person who lives in a tiny room is a monk.
5. Monk is a short form of monkey.
6. Monkeys eat bananas.
7. Bananas grow on trees.

    THEREFORE, money grows on trees.

LOUIS PHILLIPS

MIND BENDERS

My first is in mud but not in bog,
My second's in wood and also in log.
My third is in yours, but not in mine,
My fourth is in sun, and also in shine.
My fifth is in here, and also in there,
And when you're not around I run everywhere.
What am I?

OIC

I'm in a 10der mood today
& feel poetic, 2;
4 fun I'll just — off a line
& send it off 2 U.

I'm sorry you've been 6 o long;
Don't B disconsol8;
But bear your ills with 42de,
& they won't seem so gr8.

My first is in head, but not in arm;
My second is in field, but not in farm;
My third is in true and also in brave;
My fourth is in rescue, but not in save;
My whole is a creature sprightly and gay
And lives on the mountains, far away!

A river will do this, though shallow, though deep;
Turn it around and it likes eating sheep.

WILLARD R. ESPY

My first is in peapod but not in a bean.
My next is in orange but not tangerine.
My third is in eggplant and also in grape.
My fourth is in trifle but not found in crêpe.
My fifth is in rhubarb and also in rice.
My last is in yogurt but never in spice.
My whole is before you,
Plain as nose on your face.
Reason this rhyme out
And you'll win the race.

JOHN KITCHING

54

BELAGCHOLLY DAYS

Chilly Dovebber with his boadigg blast
    Dow cubs add strips the bedow add the lawd,
Eved October's suddy days are past —
      Add Subber's gawd!

I kdow dot what it is to which I cligg
    That stirs to sogg add sorrow, yet I trust
That still I sigg, but as the liddets sigg —
      Because I bust.

Farewell, by cherished strolliggs od the sward,
    Greed glades and forest shades, farewell to you;
With sorrowing heart I, wretched add forlord,
      Bid you — achew!!!

ANON

YY U R
YY U B
I C U R YY 4 ME

1-1 was a racehorse
2-2 was 1, 2
1-1 1 a race
2-2 1 1, 2.

Timothy Titus took two tees,
To tie two tups* to two tall trees
To frighten the terrible Thomas a Tattamus!
Tell me how many T's there are in that?

*tup is another word for ram

56

RIDDLE ME WRONG

My first is in scare but not in fright.
My second in spooky, no, that's not right.
My third is in riddle but not in ree.
My fourth's in the fog and I'm all at sea.
I can't find my fifth, just lost my first
Of all the puzzles this seems the worst.
I'll make a new start, a brand new riddle
Lose the whole thread, get stuck in the middle.
My first has gone bonkers, my second's gone West
Forget the whole business, that'll be best.

DAVID HARMER

The beginning of eternity,
The end of time and space,
The beginning of every end,
And the end of every place.

58

WHERE?

Where do you hide a leaf?
in, if possible, a forest.

where do you hide a wind?
among straw in dust.

where do you hide a horse?
within cloth or sea.

where do you hide the sun?
behind clouds, under horizons.

where do you hide water?
below a terrible flood.

where do you hide a storm?
inside a ghost or magician.

where do you hide a word?

DAVE CALDER

Index of First Lines and Titles

Titles are in italics. Where the title and the first line are the same, the first line only is listed.

Answers

p23:   FUNEX? Have you any eggs?
SIFX Yes, I have eggs.
FUNEM? Have you any ham?
SIFM Yes, I have ham.
ILFM'NX I'll have ham and eggs.

p24:   A man is sitting on a stool holding a leg of ham. In comes a dog and runs away with the ham. the man jumps up, picks up the stool and throws it after the dog to make him bring back the ham.

p25:   An egg turns into a silkworm, which then spins itself a cocoon and finally emerges as a moth.

p25:   It is a thorn.

p39:   I saw a fishpond, all on fire
I saw a house, bow to a squire
I saw a parson, . . . etc.

p52:   A mouse

p53:   A deer
Flow, which reversed becomes Wolf

p54:   Poetry

p56:   Too wise you are,
Too wise you be,
I see you are too wise for me

p57:   The letter E

p59:   To hide a word, don't write it down.